S CORPOR

BEGINNᴇᴋꜱ 2024

The Most Updated Guide on Starting, Growing, and Running

your S Corporation and Save on Taxes as a Small Business

Owner

Thomas Newton

Table of Contents

Introduction

An S Corporation, otherwise called an S subchapter, is a type of corporation that adheres to particular Internal Revenue Code regulations. Without paying federal corporate taxes, it may distribute income to shareholders (along with other deductions, credits, and losses). The S Corporation status, typically associated with small businesses (those with fewer than 100 shareholders), effectively provides a business with the benefits of incorporation while retaining the tax-exempt status of a partnership.

This makes an S Corporation, which is so-called because it must pay taxes under Subchapter S of the Internal Revenue Code, an advantageous option for many business organizations, especially small businesses. While it comes with a few limitations, such as rigid requirements, the advantages of S Corporation certainly outweigh the disadvantages for small-medium organizations.

However, it is a completely alien subject to many people outside the business world. Besides, the concept can sometimes seem complicated to laymen and young entrepreneurs, as they often find the pieces of information about S Corporations somewhat inaccessible. Even when you surf the web for information on S Corporation, what is obtainable leaves much to be desired. This book aims to address this gap by providing an updated guide on how to start, and grow, your S Corporation. If you are a small-medium entrepreneur planning a startup in Texas or any other place in the US, this book was intended for you.

The book dissects S Corporation from its skin down to the bone marrow. In other words, it provides a background to the subject, including a comprehensive definition of the concept as well as its benefits and disadvantages. Perhaps you have been wondering whether an S corporation rather than a C Corporation is for you or otherwise. You have probably been wondering how you can save money through S Corporation. Also, you have imagined whether it is worth the hype. With this book, you are going to become better armed to make an informed decision.

You will learn about other types of companies, their pros and cons, and how they differ from S Corporations. The details in this chapter will be useful to people who are just considering going into business and are undecided about the type of company that is best for them.

If you have made up your mind about forming an S Corporation, Chapter 8 is one useful topic you will find indispensable. It is right in the heart of the book. It highlights the S Corporation's mistakes and ways through which you can avoid them. You may need to take the time to read this chapter many times over.

Because S Corporation has a lot to do with taxes and taxation, this book will help you improve your knowledge of taxation. For example, it provides useful details about how tax deductions and credits affect your business tax rate. It also shows how you can handle your business taxes without making mistakes that can lead to conflict with the government. Best of all, you get the benefit of learning about tax breaks and deduction tactics as a small business.

I have decided to make my writing as easy to read as possible, albeit the technicalities surrounding the subject. This book is a guide that endeavors to achieve its aim through two methods. First, the majority of the contents are exposition in nature, revealing everything about S Corporation. Secondly, the book provides a step-by-step guide on how anyone can set up S Corporation without any glitches.

As such, I have attempted to break down complex topics using easily digestible language. The presentation of the topics and ideas was not designed for business gurus. Rather it aims to help small business owners in their journey towards succeeding and becoming gurus in the nearest possible future.

In short, S Corporations can be a powerful tax planning tool for small businesses. The benefits include the elimination of self-employment tax and the elimination of corporate income tax. This brief book discusses everything you need to know about S Corporations, especially how they can create value for your small business. I hope you find this book helpful and that it will help you make an informed decision. Let's get started!

Chapter 1: Explanation of S Corporations

What is S Corporation?

S Corporations are a popular choice for privately held small and medium-sized businesses. This structure is more difficult to set up than private companies or partnerships, and it frequently necessitates the assistance of a lawyer and an accountant. This raises the associated costs, both in terms of development and maintenance. One option for lowering compliance costs is first to form an LLC (which we will discuss shortly) and then elect S Corporation tax status. The best thing about an S Corporation is that you must pay yourself a reasonable salary (which is subject to FICA tax) as the owner. Nonetheless, the remainder of the company's profits is subject only to income tax, not FICA tax.

S Corporations are held to higher standards than other types of companies. In general, you must be an individual to own an S Corporation (and a U.S. resident or citizen). This is a barrier for companies seeking corporate or foreign investors (e.g., start-ups seeking venture capital funding). Although trusts and estates can own S Corporations, partnerships and corporations cannot. Profits and distributions are also rigid: they must always be allocated according to ownership.

Losses may be restricted in their use. In some cases, an S Corporation owner with losses may be unable to deduct them on their tax return. This would be carried forward to the following year, but most new businesses would welcome the extra cash from a tax refund now, not later! Such losses are usually easier to claim as a partnership or sole proprietorship.

One benefit of incorporating as an S Corp is reduced self-employment taxes. This taxable entity status has two components: salary and distribution. The self-employment tax applies to only one component of an S Corp: salary. Lower self-employment taxes may assist you in lowering your overall tax liability. Consider sole proprietorships, partnerships, and limited liability corporations as alternatives. In these cases, the business's total net income triggers self-employment taxes. Because of this, whether you keep the profits or not, you still have to pay self-employment taxes.

The second benefit is that the distributions to shareholders or owners are not taxed. An S Corp can provide significant tax savings because it can distinguish between salary and distribution components of income. If you intend to use this division to reduce your taxes, a good rule is to withdraw approximately 60% of your company's net income as salary; otherwise, the IRS may investigate your company for potential tax evasion.

This business entity can also live independently. What does this mean exactly? Well, other business types are connected to the death or exit of the owners from the business. On the other hand, an S Corp is independent of its owners. It will survive whether the owners stay, leave, or die. Due to its independence, it is an ideal business structure for long-term growth and longevity.

The third benefit of establishing an S Corp is liability protection. In certain circumstances, you will never be personally liable for your company's debts. When another type of business entity fails, the creditors or claimants of that entity have no recourse against your assets.

The fourth advantage is ownership transfer. If you leave the company, you will find it much easier to transfer your ownership than with other business entities. You can take one of two approaches. The first option is to sell your stock outright, in which ownership is immediately transferred to the buyer in exchange for monetary considerations. The second method of transferring ownership is a gradual sale. This option entails selling your stock in the company over a set period. Consider it like a payment or amortization schedule. Whatever option you choose, the entire ownership transfer process must be formalized with a printed and signed sales agreement.

The last advantage of forming an S Corp is credibility. Because this business entity is well-known among many prospective investors, customers, and vendors, forming an S Corp may provide your company with increased market credibility.

However, while an S Corporation may be the best business structure for certain purposes and the best entity solution for particular business concerns, there are some limitations to be aware of. These include:

- Restrictions on S Corporation ownership eligibility and shareholder number.

- More than 100 shareholders are not permitted in an S Corporation.

- Non-US residents are not permitted to be shareholders in an S Corporation.

Other corporate legal entities, such as C Corporations, LLCs, LPs, and certain trusts, are not permitted to be S Corporation shareholders. However, bankruptcy estates, death estates, and certain tax-exempt organizations may own S Corporation shares.

- **Restriction on the stock class of an S Corporation**: Furthermore, an S Corporation may have no more than one class of stock.

- **Restriction on an S Corporation's ability to choose its tax year:** Except for a few exceptions, an S Corporation must generally use a calendar year as its tax year. A calendar tax year is 12 consecutive months beginning January 1 and ending December 31.

Additional Compliance Requirements for Employee Payments

An S Corporation may pay its shareholder-employees a reasonable salary and periodic distributions. The S Corporation, on the other hand, pays payroll taxes on employee salaries. As a result, S Corporations will sometimes disguise them as corporate distributions to avoid paying payroll taxes on employee salaries. In response, the IRS thoroughly investigates how S Corporations pay their employees (particularly shareholder-employees).

As a result, to discourage and prevent employee salaries from being disguised as distributions in S Corporations, the IRS has enacted the following compliance rules:

1. The salary must be fair.

2. A reasonable salary must be paid before any distributions are made.

3. Even distributions (profits and losses) to S Corporation shareholders must be allocated based on each shareholder's percentage ownership of the S Corporation.

Based on the preceding, an S Corporation faces a high risk of IRS audit due to the IRS's interest in discouraging, preventing, and penalizing the compliance mentioned above.

The S Status of an S Corporation is not indefinite. The IRS has the authority to terminate it for a cause.

Another significant limitation of the S Corporation is that the S Status (basically, flow-through taxation) can be lost if even one shareholder transfers their S Corporation shares to an owner who is not legally permitted to own shares in an S Corporation (e.g., transfers the S Corporation's to a non-US resident). If the S Corporation status is lost, the S Corporation reverts to a regular C Corporation and is taxed from that point forward. Furthermore, the now-reverted C Corporation will be barred from filing another S Corporation election for the next five years.

- S Corporations, like C Corporations, must be registered with the state and are more costly to form.

- Administrative duties are required; S Corporations are subject to more restrictions on stock issuance than C Corporations.

- Estates, individuals, and trustees are the only types of stockholders.

- The company cannot offer paid fringe benefits; it is expensive to establish and has ongoing expenses such as franchise tax fees.

- Unlike other business entities, you must be a legal resident of the United States.

- Ownership is limited because there can't be more than 100 shareholders.

Annual shareholder meetings are one example of a corporate formality to consider.

The IRS Form 2553 must be submitted when converting your company to an S Corporation. It could be beneficial for a company that needs a corporate structure with tax flexibility similar to that of a sole proprietorship. All states do not recognize it; it is only valid within the United States.

Chapter 2: Is an S Corporation the Correct Decision for Me?

Deciding to form an S Corporation will benefit you in various ways, most of which have been discussed in the previous chapter.

While avoiding self-employment tax may sound appealing, shareholders in an S Corporation must pay themselves reasonable compensation, subject to Social Security and Medicare taxes. What exactly is adequate remuneration? In general, you would compute that based on several factors.

The taxation process is the only distinction between a C Corporation and an S Corporation. While a C Corporation is subject to double taxation (corporate tax and personal income tax on shareholders), an S Corporation is subject to pass-through taxation, which means that profits and losses are passed through to the owners' tax returns. S Corporations must file their taxes annually, whereas C Corporations must file quarterly.

An S Corporation can enjoy tax benefits similar to a traditional corporation while avoiding disadvantages. You must meet IRS requirements and have no more than 100 shareholders to qualify for S Corporation status. S Corporations must also pay a yearly fee based on their revenue. S Corporations are easier to acquire than traditional corporations because partners can own them. The main advantage of an S Corporation is that it can benefit from a corporate income tax reduction. Revenue can be taxed individually and treated as a partnership, making this a viable option for assisting small businesses in growing and receiving income.

The Operating Agreement for an S Corporation

As hinted earlier, to elect to be taxed as an S Corporation, the entity must file Form 2553. (Election by a Small Business Corporation). The timing of this election is where things get a little complicated. Small business corporations must make the election either during the previous taxable year or before the 15th day of the third month of any taxable year.

When an entity chooses S Corporation status, it keeps it until the election is revoked. When an entity chooses S Corporation status, it keeps it until the election is revoked. At least one-half of the corporation's shareholders must agree to the S termination Corporation's methods:

- The revocation is retroactive to the first day of the corporation's tax year if made by the 15th day of the third month.

- If made after the 15th day of the third month, the revocation takes effect on the first day of the following tax year.

- The corporation revokes the election by filing a statement stating that it has done so.

This is where things get tricky. The Small Business Act of 1996 authorized the Internal Revenue Service for the first time to grant relief to entities that filed an election after the deadline. If the Service determines that there was reasonable cause for the failure to hold a timely election, the S election will be valid. This was a significant change in S Corporation law.

There are three ways to seek relief for submitting a late S election today. The first option is for the corporation to seek relief under Rev. Proc. Rev. Proc. 2007-62 2003-43 if it can show that it had good reason for failing to make a timely S election and meet certain deadlines. Assume the IRS fails to notify a corporation of a problem within six months of the due date for filing a timely S Corporation return for the first year the corporation intended to be an S Corporation. In that case, the corporation may file a request for relief under Rev. Proc. 97-48. The third method of requesting relief is through a private letter ruling.

Suppose the corporation's stock is issued to a nonresident alien, a non-qualified trust, another corporation, a partnership, more than the permitted shareholders, or more than one class of stock. In that case, the S election is statutorily revocable. Furthermore, the election can be revoked if the corporation's passive investment income exceeds 25% of gross receipts for three years.

Relief for an S Corporation that unintentionally revokes its election by failing to meet the requirements of a small business corporation or failing the passive income test. If the Service determines that the termination was made inadvertently, steps were taken to correct the cause within a reasonable time of discovery, and the corporation and each shareholder agree to the Service's adjustments, the Service may grant relief.

S Corporations can be challenging to comprehend. The important point to remember is that once you've made your decision, it must be carefully monitored by a professional. To obtain S Corporation status, a company must meet specific IRS requirements. Among these qualifications are the following:

- Being incorporated domestically (within the U.S.).

- Shareholders who meet certain eligibility criteria.

- Have only one type of stock.

- A maximum of one hundred shareholders.

Individuals, specific estates and trusts, and tax-exempt organizations (501(c)(3) are all eligible to be S corporation shareholders. Corporations, partnerships, and non-resident aliens are not permitted to participate as shareholders.

How to Apply to Become an S Corporation

- Enter your company name and address.

- Enter your business's EIN. We obtained your employer identification number (EIN) from the IRS. It's a 9-digit number.

- Enter the Date Incorporated as the date on your company's charter.

- Input the state of incorporation. It is the state in which your business is registered.

- Enter your first, last, and job title.

- Enter your phone number here.

- Enter your first and last name, as well as your street address.

- Date and sign

- Check the entire form for accuracy before printing.

- Fill in your title, date, and signature.

You've completed your task. The IRS will review your request and send you a letter indicating whether it is approved. The letter of determination should arrive within 60 days. If you haven't received the letter within 60 days, you can call the IRS at 1-800-829-4933 to find out where it is. Once you receive the IRS determination letter stating that your company is approved to be treated as an S Corporation, it is officially an S Corporation. You can pay salaries, run payroll, file S Corporation tax, etc.

Dear Entrepreneur,

Thank you for your purchase!

We extend our sincere gratitude for choosing

"S-Corporations for Beginners"

as a part of your reading repertoire

Scan this QR-CODE to get your

4 FREE BONUS resources

thoughtfully curated to elevate your knowledge of

effective communication at work, leadership,

time management, and overcoming procrastination.

Your commitment to enhancing your small business acumen is
commendable, and we are here to support your journey.

Warm regards,

Thomas

Chapter 3: Difference between S Corporations and Other Types of Company

Deciding on the right business structure is crucial to the success of all businesses. The previous chapters provided an in-depth exposition on S Corporation, highlighting the advantages and disadvantages and other important things small business owners should know. You have also been exposed to the requirements for starting an S Corporation. However, it is not the ultimate business structure. It is instructive for every entrepreneur to ruminate on the business structure that serves their interest best. This chapter examines other types of businesses in relation to an S Corporation. The expositions presented on these types of companies will help to highlight how each differs from S Corporation. Let's start with Sole Proprietorship.

Sole Proprietorship

This means that a single person will manage your company. This is a popular option for small businesses. Although it is a simple and low-cost business structure, it increases your liability and costs you significant tax benefits.

With this structure, you cannot pay yourself a salary. Instead, you will withdraw profits as needed. Every year, whether you have withdrawn the profits, you must pay personal income tax on the entire taxable profits of the company.

Remember that most benefits are subject to federal income tax and Social Security and Medicare taxes (or "FICA"). Many small business owners pay FICA taxes in addition to income taxes.

Sole proprietorships are intended for small, single-owned businesses (small service businesses, food stands, freelancers, consultants, etc.)

Because sole proprietors lack stock or ownership units, the only way to exit is to sell the company's assets.

Pros of Sole Proprietorship

- It is simple to get started because there is no registration required.

- Decisions can be made quickly because there is no need for consultation.

- No double taxation exists because the business and the owner are treated as one entity; thus, business income is reported on a personal income tax return.

- Only the income generated by the business is taxed.

- If the business makes a profit, the owner gets to keep it because they are the sole proprietor.

Cons of Sole Proprietorship

- Unlimited liability means that if the company cannot pay its debts and liabilities, the owner's assets, such as your car or home, can be used to make the difference.

- Social Security and Medicare taxes are double what you would pay as an employee.

- If the company suffers losses, the owner is solely responsible.

- Because there is no separation between you and the business, obtaining a business loan from a lender is difficult.

Most startups are sole proprietorships due to the ease with which they can be established. Unfortunately, unlimited liability exists because there is no separation between the owner and the business, which can be extremely dangerous. As a result, most of these businesses convert to LLCs or corporations.

Sole Proprietorship versus S Corporation in a nutshell: The major difference between Sole Proprietorship and S Corporation is that the latter has the privilege of limited liability protection while the former does not. Also, the business owner of an S Corporation pays income tax and FICA on their "reasonable salary" and only income taxes on distributions, while his counterpart in a sole proprietorship pays income taxes on the net profit of the business and self-employment taxes.

Partnership

A partnership is like a sole proprietorship in that it has multiple owners. In most cases, extraordinarily little (or no) paperwork is required to establish and maintain a partnership.

Because of this, many small businesses are formed as partnerships. Although the paperwork requirements are minimal, multi-owner companies are inherently more complicated, so at least one partnership operating agreement that governs the business's operations and ownership is strongly recommended.

Only in the case of partnerships is it not necessary to allocate the firm's income proportionally to ownership. This flexibility can be beneficial when a silent partner has contributed most of the capital but does not expect a comparable share of the profits. A partnership agreement should clearly state any such arrangement.

In short, this structure is commonly used by small, new businesses that have yet to achieve true profitability. This is particularly relevant for small businesses with no employees, where the owners do most of the work (perhaps in your case?)

While the structure is advantageous, there are liability risks. You are equally liable for your partner's mistakes because of how a partnership is structured. Many partnerships fail because they form with people close to them and cannot handle disagreements. As a result, you should proceed with caution before forming a partnership.

A general partnership is simple to establish. There is no need to file any forms. All that is required is a verbal agreement. However, recording your agreement in a legal document is a good idea. In a legal dispute, this partnership agreement will prevent many problems.

Partnership Agreements

The partnership agreements function like the bylaws of a corporation. Here's what the agreement should establish:

- The name of your partnership.

- How profits and responsibilities will be shared.

- How losses will be shared.

- The terms of exiting and entering the partnership.

- The different sections of the agreement need to describe the following items at a minimum:

- The nature of your business.

- The partnership's establishment date and its expiry date.

- The duties that every partner will be expected to undertake.

- The amount of capital and resources each partner will contribute to the partnership.

- The rules of dissolution of the partnership.

How will disagreements be resolved along with the proper procedure and documentation?

A lawyer should handle all partnership-related paperwork. Because each business has unique requirements, it is best to tailor the agreement to your specific needs. The most significant advantage of forming a partnership is that it is less formal than forming a corporation or a limited liability partnership (LLP).

As with sole proprietorships, all partnership income is considered personal, so you must only pay taxes once. This could result in a lower tax bill than forming a corporation would. However, there are some significant drawbacks to consider.

I've already mentioned how you'll be held accountable for the mistakes of others. However, it is not only incorrect but also indebted. If your business partner makes a bad decision and borrows more money than your partnership can afford, your creditors will not distinguish between you and your partner; you're both equally liable.

A partnership is not the best business structure for a freight brokerage. It may be more practical for you to incorporate as a sole prop and collaborate with your partner, who may also incorporate as a sole prop (if forming a corporation together is not an option).

Pros of Partnership

- **Easy to start** – It's easy to start since it doesn't require registration. If the business incurs losses, it's divided by the partners, and the burden is shared.

- **Less capital required** – All the partners contribute towards raising the capital rather than raising it alone.

- **Consultation** – There must be consultation among the partners if a decision needs to be made, ensuring they make the best decision.

- **Less business loss** - The business losses can be deducted from the partner's tax returns.

- **No double taxation** – the business and owners are viewed as one; hence the business income is reported on each partner's income tax return.

Cons of Partnership

- **Unlimited liability** – The partners remain liable for the business debts and liabilities. If the business cannot repay its debts, the partners' assets can be used to settle the debts.

- **Issues between partners** - Disputes among the partners could negatively affect the business.

- **Partner liability** - In some states, the partners are liable for each other's careless behavior.

- **Hard to get loans** - Obtaining loans for a business that lacks registration is difficult.

Startups form partnerships primarily to reduce the risks associated with starting a business independently. They provide an excellent support system, but you should be cautious about who you partner with.

Partnership versus S Corporation in a nutshell: A partnership does not require the partners to do any paperwork with the government or fill any form. On the other hand, the formation of an S Corporation is a lot more complex, with specific requirements spelled out. The main steps you will need to take to apply for an S Corporation have been highlighted in the previous chapter. In addition, the structure of an S corporation is not as flexible as a partnership. In terms of key decision-making, for instance, all partners in a partnership have an equal say in every business decision. However, a board is elected in an S Corporation, enjoying the privilege of voting for or against any major business issues.

C Corporations

Because the C Corporation structure is generally preferred for complex and large businesses, it will not be your first choice. These are the country's largest corporations, accounting for roughly half of all business profits in the United States despite accounting for only about 5% of all businesses.

Let's review its main characteristics to understand how it differs from other business types.

C Corporations comprise all large publicly traded companies in the United States. Private C Corporations are unusual and are typically formed for reasons other than taxation. One company that uses the C Corporation structure is a high-growth start-up seeking serial financing. They are compelled to take this route because their intended investors may be foreign entities or individuals who cannot invest in an S Corporation. The main difference between C Corporations is that they pay income taxes.

The main disadvantage of this structure is that C Corporation shareholders must usually pay taxes on corporate dividends. So, first and foremost, the C Corporation is required to pay income taxes. The remaining funds are then distributed to the owners, who must again pay taxes. This is referred to as double taxation.

This double taxation discourages private companies from using the C Corporation structure. What about another disadvantage? Losses from a C Corporation cannot be deducted from a stockholder's other personal income.

Pros of C Corporations

- The owners, who are the shareholders, are not liable for the Corporation's debts and liabilities.

- Corporations are entitled to more tax breaks than other types of business entities.

- Corporations can raise more capital by selling stock on the stock market.

- A Corporation's ownership is easily transferable, which means that if the owners believe the business will fail, they can sell it without losing their capital investment.

- Employees benefit from not paying taxes on health insurance premiums and life insurance, which are fully deductible as corporate expenses.

Cons of C Corporations

- A corporation is more expensive to establish than other types of business entities.

- Double taxation exists because the corporation and the shareholder's income are taxed on dividends.

- When forming a corporation, a lot of paperwork is involved, including legal paperwork that must be filed with the Secretary of State.

- The shareholders have no say in how the corporation operates.

- Because the directors must be consulted, decision-making takes time.

- Losses incurred by the business cannot be deducted from the owners' tax returns.

- Many corporate formalities exist, such as shareholder meetings and by-laws.

Because of the complexities involved, most startups do not choose to form a corporation, but as your business grows, it provides more legal protections.

C Corporation versus S Corporation in a nutshell:

Both C Corporation and S Corporation derive their names from the Internal Revenue Code under which they are taxed. S Corporations are taxed under Subchapter S, while C Corporations are taxed under the Subchapter C of the IRS Code. Taxation is the major yardstick for drawing a difference between these two entities. While an S Corporation enjoys pass-through taxation, a C Corporation is a separately taxed entity. Nonetheless, the different entities can be differentiated by considering shareholders' restrictions. While C Corporations do not have shareholder restrictions, an S Corporation cannot have more than 100 shareholders.

Limited Liability Company (LLC)

The IRS does not recognize an LLC as a taxpaying business structure; instead, it is a legal entity only. This means that the owners of an LLC must choose one of the other structures discussed above as their tax identity.

At the same time, LLC structures have additional advantages. Limited Liability Companies, for example, help protect the owner's assets from a business lawsuit, in contrast to sole proprietorships and partnerships. Without an LLC, a sole proprietor or partner may become personally liable for a lawsuit or judgment that exceeds the business's assets, potentially exposing the owner's assets to a claim. A "limited liability" corporation cannot do this.

What else is there to say? In general, the structure of an LLC is simpler to manage than an S or C Corporation. True corporations, for example, are required to hold annual meetings and keep minutes of those meetings. An LLC taxed as a corporation is typically exempt from these rules.

Furthermore, a company that starts as an LLC has the option of changing its entity later on. So, once your business is profitable, you can form an LLC taxed as a partnership and then convert to an S Corporation.

Most of the time, the LLC umbrella does not affect taxes. An LLC owner must decide whether the business should be a C or S Corporation, a sole proprietorship, or a partnership for tax purposes.

LLCs are a popular business structure for small businesses because they provide flexibility, limited liability protection, and a potentially lower tax bill. This entity operates in the state like a corporation but is taxed by the federal government like a partnership or sole proprietorship. It offers its owners the same limited liability protection as a corporation while avoiding double taxation by passing earnings through to them. When members of an LLC file their income tax returns, they are taxed only once.

Because LLCs are formed at the state level, the laws governing their formation differ. There are no limitations on the number of members an LLC can have. These companies don't need a board of directors or even multiple members. A single-member LLC can be formed.

The procedure for forming an LLC is straightforward. You can hire an agent or apply directly to the state secretary's office. You must register your company and file your articles of incorporation. This document serves as the operating manual for your LLC. In the case of single-member LLCs, it isn't particularly important. If you have more than one member, you should have a lawyer draft this agreement because it can significantly impact your revenue split and other operational issues.

Along with your articles, you must draft an operating agreement outlining how you and your partners will run the LLC daily. One of the members is usually designated as the managing member and oversees the LLC's operations. Although many states do not require operating agreements, drafting one is a good idea in case of future disagreements is a good idea.

LLCs can hire employees, but they must first obtain an EIN from the IRS. Some states will require you to place an ad in the newspaper announcing the formation of your LLC after you have filed your agreement and articles with the state. Check with your county office to see which publications are appropriate for this.

Unlike sole proprietorships, raising funds with an LLC is simple, though not as simple as with a corporation. Due to the inability of LLCs to issue shares, an investor becomes a member rather than a shareholder. While membership is a good option for new investors, cashing out the money can be difficult (Zarzycki, 2020). I'll get to this right away.

An LLC's most appealing feature is that it protects its owners from liability while also allowing you to reduce your overall tax bill. When forming an LLC, you should open a separate bank account to hold the company's funds. If you do not do this, you may expose your assets to liability litigation. If you operate the LLC from your personal bank account, it can be used as evidence that your assets are also involved in the litigation, and the LLC's protection is null and void.

Pros of LLC

The tax advantages of forming an LLC do not end with single taxation. You can file as a C or S Corporation if filing as an LLC does not result in a lower tax bill. Your LLC will be required to pay corporate taxes in this case. LLCs are extremely adaptable, with every aspect of their operation customizable to meet your specific needs. Whether it's a change in how profits are distributed to members or a change in the operating agreement, you can do it all with little effort.

If you have employees, you can elect to be taxed as an S corporation to avoid paying self-employment taxes. Therefore, limited liability companies (LLCs) are popular among freight brokers. They are ideal for a beginner because they provide the flexibility and credibility you need to present to your clients.

- Limited liability means that the owners are not personally liable for the debts or liabilities of the company.

- Members can instruct the IRS on whether their LLC should be taxed as a partnership or corporation.

- Establishing an LLC is simple because it only requires filing with the Secretary of State.

- Members are not personally liable for their fellow members' irresponsible behavior.

- There is no double taxation because it is imposed on the personal or corporate level, but not both.

Cons of LLC

LLCs have a few drawbacks. The most significant disadvantage is how a departing member is treated. Assume an investor wishes to withdraw funds; dealing with this situation can be challenging. The member's shares would be purchased in the case of a corporation but not in the case of an LLC. Many states require the LLC to be dissolved, whereas others permit the departing member to be bought out.

LLCs are taxed in some states, which can be costly for some businesses. For example, a minimum tax of $300 per year is required in Delaware, regardless of whether the business makes a profit. Some investors are hesitant to invest in LLCs because of the issues with member exits.

Despite these disadvantages, LLCs are ideal for individuals who want to start a new business and eventually grow into a larger corporation. While running a corporation can be expensive, LLCs offer cost savings and all the protection you need to run your business safely.

- An LLC is more expensive to establish than a sole proprietorship or general partnership.

- Because they have unlimited liability, partners in charge of operations are liable for any debt incurred by the business.

- Any disagreements among partners are likely to have an impact on the business.

Small businesses generally prefer the limitation of Liability Companies because they combine the legal protection of corporations with sole proprietorships or partnerships.

Limited Liability Company (LLC) versus S Corporation in a nutshell: Limited Liability Company (LLC) is often discussed in the same context as an S Corporation. Therefore, many people confuse the two as options that can be chosen one against the other. However, each of them refers to separate aspects of a business. While an S Corporation is essentially a tax clarification, an LLC is a kind of business entity or a legal business structure just like a partnership or corporation. Put differently, an S Corporation is registered as either an LLC or as a C Corporation as part of its requirements.

Limited Partnership

Limited partnership business entities must register with the state, which entails filing paperwork. There are two kinds of partners in a Limited Partnership:

1. **General Partners**: The general partners own the company, run it, and bear its liabilities.

2. **Limited Partners**: Limited partners are investors who are not involved in the business's day-to-day operations. They are also known as silent partners because their liability is limited to their capital contribution.

The following are the advantages and disadvantages of forming a Limited Partnership:

Pros of Limited Partnership

- The general partners can obtain the funds required for the business while continuing to operate.

- A limited partnership is a different way to raise funds from investors without personal liability.

- The partnership must not be dissolved if a limited partner wishes to leave.

Cons of Limited Partnership

- If limited partners become unintentionally involved in business operations, they may face personal liability.

- A Limited Partnership is more expensive to form than a General Partnership.

- General partners are personally liable for the debts and liabilities of the company.

- Limited Partnerships benefit business owners with multiple businesses because they can bring in investors with limited liability.

Chapter 4: How You Can Save Money with S Corporations

S Corporations, like partnerships, are required to report their deductions and income. S Corporations must file annual information returns (Form the 1120S) to report their income, profits, deductions, losses, and tax credits. Schedule K-1 must be provided to shareholders by S Corporation owners detailing their ownership interests in the items listed on their 1120S. Stakeholders use Schedule E and individual income tax returns (Form 1040) to report their share of the corporation's loss of income.

S Corporations are distinguished from partnerships by the employment status of the company's owners. A partnership-taxed

LLC's owner is not considered a worker of the LLC. They are merely a business proprietor.

On the other hand, an S Corporation employer who performs more than minor functions for the corporation is taxed as both an employee and an owner. In effect, the owner of such a corporation typically wears two hats: shareholder (owner) and employee.

Employees and self-employed people pay the same Medicare and Social Security taxes, but they are paid differently. The employer withholds half of the total tax and deducts the other half from the employee's pay. It makes no difference if the employer pays half or not if you own a business that pays these taxes—you are the employer.

The owner/employees' efforts must be rewarded with a fair wage and any other employee benefits desired by the corporation. The employee/owner must report the S Corporation's earnings on their tax returns and pay their share of Medicare and Social Security taxes on all employee salaries. On behalf of the owner/employee, the corporation should withhold and pay federal income taxes, employment taxes, state and federal unemployment taxes, Social Security taxes, and Medicare.

Savings on Employment Taxes

Being classified as an S Corporation employee has several significant advantages. If you use the S Corporation tax procedure, you may be able to withdraw funds from your business without incurring employment taxes. This is because you are exempt from paying employment taxes on the corporation's distributions. That is, you, the owner, pay taxes on income passed through your corporation rather than being paid as an employee for your work. The lower the employment tax, the higher the distribution. S Corporations are the only business structures that allow owners to defer Medicare and Social Security taxes. This has historically been the primary reason for S Corporations' popularity.

You would owe no Medicare or Social Security taxes if you did not receive any pay. According to the IRS, S Corporation employees and shareholders must be paid a reasonable wage comparable to what comparable businesses pay for comparable services. Furthermore, an S Corporation may find it advantageous to pay large employee salaries due to pass-through tax deductions.

Tax Deduction for Pass-Through

The Tax Cuts and Jobs Act added new deductions for pass-through corporations, which include sole proprietorships, partnerships, limited liability companies, and S Corporations. Owners of these entities have been deducting approximately 20% of their income from their taxable income since 2018. This is the personal deduction that all pass-through entity owners can claim, regardless of whether they itemize.

Tax-Free Wealth

Tax-free investing is a great way to avoid looming tax increases. You can defer paying taxes on a portion of your income and assets. Aside from S Corporations, here are some other tax-advantaged strategies to consider adding to your portfolio or expanding your use if you already have them.

Capital Gains on Long-term Investments

Long-term capital gains are typically taxed at a maximum rate of 20%. Many people are unaware that the 20% tax rate only applies to those with the highest incomes. Lower income levels have lower rates. For many people, such capital gains are taxed at 0%. And the figure is less than 10% for many others. Qualified dividends should be taxed the same as ordinary dividends.

Qualified dividends and gains on sales of assets held for more than a year are taxed at 0% until they exceed the threshold amounts if taxable income other than long-term profits or dividends does not exceed $40,400 for a single taxpayer, $54,100 for household heads, or $80,800 for joint filers.

While capital gains and dividends are not taxed at the federal level, they increase adjusted gross income, which may result in higher taxes on Social Security benefits and other taxes. Furthermore, capital gains may be taxed differently in your state.

You can avoid paying taxes on long-term capital gains by managing your taxable income.

Avoid actions that will increase your gross income, such as increasing traditional IRA or 401(k) distributions. Instead, if possible, take additional distributions from tax-free accounts. If there is no urgent need to sell investments this year, you can do so next year.

You can also consider increasing your deductions and lowering your taxable income. For example, charitable contributions from multiple years can be combined into one year when itemized expenses are deducted.

Another possibility is to liquidate investments in which you have incurred paper losses. This loss is deducted from the year's capital gains. Losses more than gains of up to $3,000 may be deducted from other revenue, and any excess losses may be carried forward and used in the same manner in subsequent years.

Remember that to qualify for long-term capital gains, an asset must be held for more than a year. A one-day early asset sale results in a short-term gain taxed as regular income.

529 College Savings Plans

These savings plans are excellent estate planning tools because they provide tax-free investment returns. You contribute to the 529 plan and select a beneficiary. A child or even a grandchild is typically named beneficiary, with the expectation that the account will be used to fund a child's college education in the future.

You can use up to five years' worth of the $15,000 annual gift tax exclusion in a single year when contributing to the account. This ensures that a gift of nearly $75,000 is exempt from all gift taxes and does not deplete your lifetime estate or gift tax exclusions.

Individual Health Savings Accounts

These are the three-tiered tax strategies available, and they are an excellent way to save for retirement. Many high-deductible medical insurance policies and plans allow the insured to contribute to health savings accounts (HSAs).

Contributions are tax deductible when made personally and are tax-deductible when made by an employer up to a certain annual limit. The account can be used to make investments, and earnings accumulate tax-free.

HSA distributions are tax-free if they are used to pay or reimburse you for qualified medical expenses that are not covered by other sources. In addition, if you had unreimbursed medical expenses in previous years, the HSA may be able to reimburse you tax-free.

Every eligible person can open an HSA and contribute the maximum amount allowed annually. You must contribute if your employer does not contribute to the annual cap. Transferring funds from a taxable cash account to an HSA makes sense.

Qualified Small Business Stocks

A worthwhile investment in a small business may be tax-free up to a certain amount. A qualified small business is organized as a "C" Corporation in the United States of America. Sole proprietorships, S Corporations, and limited liability companies are not permitted.

Stock must have been issued after August 10, 1993 and acquired explicitly from the corporation in exchange for cash, property (other than stocks), or services. Additionally, the overall tax basis of the business's total gross assets must be less than $50 million when the stock is received.

401(k)s and ROTH IRAs

Transferring assets to ROTH accounts creates a long period of tax-free earnings and gains. Contributions to ROTH accounts continue to have no tax advantages. The advantages include tax-free investment returns and tax-free distributions of accumulated funds.

ROTH IRA and ROTH 401(k) contributions are permitted (k). You can also convert a traditional IRA or 401(k) to a ROTH IRA.

Life Insurance

Life insurance benefits are possibly the longest-lasting tax-free asset, and their status is unlikely to change anytime soon.

Throughout your life, you can borrow tax-free from the cash value account of most perpetual life insurance policies and the benefits payable to beneficiaries. Nonetheless, any unpaid loans reduce the number of benefits payable to beneficiaries.

Asset repositioning as life insurance might be a good idea. You could, for example, withdraw funds from a traditional IRA and then use the after-tax proceeds to purchase permanent life insurance or establish a trust for your children or grandchildren.

The guaranteed life insurance benefit will be tax-free to the beneficiaries. The life insurance gain will exceed the IRA's after-tax value for many people. It is also not subject to market fluctuations, unlike an IRA.

Other assets could be restructured as life insurance, providing beneficiaries with tax-free inheritances. Health insurance can be purchased through the marketplace and deducted as a business expense for your S Corporation. You must adhere to specific rules and regulations. If you have high-deductible health insurance, your S Corporation can contribute to your HSA as part of your employer contribution. Consult your tax advisor for more information.

Chapter 5: How to Set Up Your S Corporation

Primary Characteristics of an S Corporation

The S Corporation as a Separate Legal Entity

The S Corporation is a legal entity in and of itself. Its existence is distinct from that of its shareholders. It has its name, identity, personality, rights, and responsibilities. It also has its own IRS taxpayer account number (EIN). In short, an S Corporation is a separate legal person with all the rights and responsibilities.

The S Limited Corporation's Liability Provision

S Corporations, like C Corporations, benefit from limited liability protection. This feature (if properly implemented and enforced) will generally protect the S-shareholders Corporation from personal liability and their assets from seizure due to the S-debts Corporations and liabilities. Who can form an S Corporation and/or own shares in one?

One or more shareholders typically form an S Corporation, but no more than 100 shareholders are permitted.

In addition, S Corporations can be formed or owned by US citizens and residents. Non-US resident aliens, on the other hand, are not permitted to be shareholders in an S Corporation.

Shares of an S Corporation may also be owned by bankruptcy estates, death estates, and certain tax-exempt organizations. However, corporate legal entities (such as LLCs, C Corporations, LPs, and certain trusts) are generally not permitted to be shareholders of an S Corporation.

It is important to note that the secondary sale of an S Corporation by an eligible shareholder to a non-eligible shareholder may void the status of the S Corporation, converting it to a regular C Corporation. If this occurs, the now-reverted C Corporation cannot file another S-status election for five years.

How an S Corporation is Formed

In this case, the application would essentially be for forming a regular corporation (a C Corporation). A C Corporation is "born" after the Articles of Incorporation are approved. In other words, an S Corporation is formed from a C Corporation. Following that (and if eligible), the C Corporation may file IRS Form 2553 to elect to be taxed as an S Corporation. The C Corporation becomes an S Corporation after 2553 is approved.

The Governance Document for an S Corporation

As with the C Corporation, corporate bylaws (which should be custom-drafted) provide and govern the rights and responsibilities of the S-shareholders, corporation's directors, and officers. The corporate bylaws establish the general guidelines for the S-internal corporation's operations. If the S Corporation fails to have and maintain corporate bylaws, it may lose its limited liability protection and become subject to the state's default corporate rules.

Meetings, Minutes, and Resolutions of the S Corporation

S Corporations, like C-corporations, are required by law to hold an annual shareholders' meeting because they are corporations. Corporations (including S Corporations) must hold regular board of directors and shareholder meetings. Meeting minutes and any resolutions reached during such meetings must be documented and kept as part of the S-business corporation's records.

The Management Structure of an S Corporation

The management structure of an S Corporation is similar to that of a C-corporation in that a board of directors and officers manages it. The shareholders of an S Corporation elect the board of directors to oversee the corporation. The directors also appoint the officers who oversee the day-to-day operations of the S Corporation. A single shareholder can serve as the corporation's sole director and officer in a single-shareholder S Corporation (or C-corporation) (where allowed under state law).

The Reliance of S Corporations on Corporate Formalities

The directors and officers of an S Corporation must also treat the S Corporation as a separate, distinct, and independent legal entity and thus must adhere to corporate formalities. Again, suppose the corporation's officers, directors, and shareholders fail to have, keep, and comply with corporate bylaws. In that case, the S Corporation will most likely lose its limited liability protection feature (thus exposing the shareholders, directors, officers, and their assets to risk). The S Corporation may also become subject to the state's default corporate rules.

As you can see, the S Corporation provides two of the most important and desired features in a business structure: limited liability protection and flow-through taxation. However, the S Corporation has numerous shareholder restrictions (such as no nonresident shareholders; generally, no corporate entity shareholders; and no more than 100 shareholders, etc.).

To make matters worse, an S Corporation may lose its S-status due to a shareholder-eligibility violation. If it does, it may not file another S-status election for five years.

In short, the limited liability company (LLC) was legislatively accepted and introduced in the United States in part to address and amend the limitations mentioned above. As a result, the LLC has more expansive and inclusive ownership/shareholder eligibility standards (which the S Corporation does not have), and the two most-desired S Corporation features limited liability protection and flow-through taxation.

Employee Fringe Benefits and the S Corporation

An S Corporation may provide pre-tax health insurance to its employees. It may also offer health insurance to its employee-shareholders (S Corporation shareholders who are also S Corporation employees). The health insurance premiums the S Corporation pays its shareholders are deductible business expenses. It also counts as income for the individual shareholder. Furthermore, an S Corporation does not provide a medical-reimbursement plan to cover its employees' additional medical expenses.

Privacy and S Corporation

It is possible to structure a corporation (including an S Corporation), so its ownership information is concealed. When providing owner anonymity, the corporation is an effective vehicle for doing so. However, it will primarily be determined by the jurisdiction in which the corporation is formed. In some jurisdictions, the incorporation process allows corporations' ownership information to remain anonymous or difficult to discover. Nominee directors and officers, for example, can be used to register a corporation in Wyoming and Nevada (C or S). This effectively keeps such corporations' true ownership information anonymous and private.

Ownership anonymity provides privacy and security while protecting the S Corporation and its shareholders from frivolous lawsuits. It can also be used to combat harassment and stalking.

Credibility and Acceptance of S Corporation

A corporation (S or C) is a common and well-known business structure that is widely accepted by the public and the business world. The corporation is a well-established, tried-and-true business structure. No other business structure outperforms the corporation regarding public credibility, familiarity, and acceptance. As a result, doing business as a corporation (S or C) can help to bridge the credibility and trust gap with the public quickly.

Transferability of S Corporation Shares

S Corporation shares can generally be transferred (sold or gifted). S Corporation stock can be freely transferred without a restricting or encumbering provision in the S-bylaws corporations or an existing buy-sell agreement.

If a buy-sell agreement exists, it will specify the terms and conditions under which an S Corporation shareholder may sell, buy, or otherwise transfer their S Corporation shares. Assume no existing buy-sell agreement or contrary provisions in the S-bylaws exist. In that case, the corporation's stock of the S Corporation may be freely bought, sold, or otherwise transferred.

However, suppose the transfer of the S-stock corporation results in a violation of the Internal Revenue Code's S Corporation rules (by the S Corporation). In that case, the S Corporation will lose its S-status automatically. For example, if an S-stock corporation is sold to a non-US resident alien (knowingly or unknowingly), the S-S-status corporation will be terminated. This is because non-US resident aliens are prohibited from owning stock in an S Corporation. The S Corporation will then be converted to a C Corporation (its former status).

What is the Procedure for Transferring S Corporation Stock?

1. Assume there are relevant provisions in the S-bylaws of the corporation or a buy-sell agreement. In that case, the stock transfer procedures outlined in the relevant document must be strictly adhered to.

2. To memorialize the terms of the transfer, you will typically need to draft a stock-transfer agreement. The stock can be sold in exchange for money or gifted to another person for no monetary or other consideration.

3. The parties should then sign the stock-transfer agreement. If the transaction is a purchase, the seller will sign the stock

certificate, and the buyer will pay the seller. If the stock transfer certificate is a gift, the owner simply signs it and gives it to the recipient.

4. The secretary of the board of directors should then record the stock transfer in the S-stock corporation's ledger.

5. Make and have the new stockholder sign a document agreeing to the corporation being taxed as an S Corporation. The contract must be both signed and notarized.

One of the requirements for receiving and maintaining S-status is that all S-shareholder corporations must consent (in signed writing) to the corporation being taxed as an S Corporation. The consent should then be recorded in the S Corporation's business records.

Prospects for Taking the Company Public in the Future

C-corporation shares are preferred by public investors more than any other business structure. They specifically prefer Delaware C Corporations. Due to tax law and the structure of their governing documents, venture capitalists cannot invest in S Corporations.

Furthermore, because the S Corporation has a shareholder limit of 100, conducting a meaningful IPO in which the company's shares are supposed to be made available to hundreds of thousands, if not millions, of shareholders is nearly impossible. As a result, an S Corporation is unsuitable if you intend to seek significant external financing or to conduct your corporation's initial public offering (IPO).

However, it is possible to begin operating as an S Corporation and, whenever you want to prepare for external financing or an IPO, revoke your corporation's S-status and begin operating as a C Corporation.

Real Estate Investing with an S Corporation

The S Corporation offers no additional benefits to the average passive real estate investor. However, it may be useful to real estate operators whose primary business is real estate.

An S Corporation does not always assist in lowering self-employment tax.

Real estate investing is not commonly considered a viable business or trade. Profits from real estate investing are thus exempt from self-employment tax. They are only subject to income tax (perhaps net investment income tax).

This means that, in most cases, a typical real estate investor (i.e., a passive investor whose real estate activities do not constitute a trade or business) does not have to pay self-employment tax. This also implies that if a typical passive real estate investor used an S Corporation, the investor would not be merely reducing their self-employment tax liability.

Chapter 6: Shareholder Distributions

A shareholder in an S Corporation is a complicated concept. The basis is important to understand because if an S Corporation incurs a loss, a shareholder cannot accept the loss if it exceeds the basis. Simply put, the basis is the value of your corporation's stock shares. Simply put, the basis is the amount of money invested in the corporation by the owner. Assume you set up an S Corporation and deposit $1,000 into the company's checking account before you start a business. Your initial investment is $1,000. You will almost certainly lend money to the company to keep it operating while doing business. Debt basis can be confusing when discussing the S Corporation basis; however, it is an essential concept for you to understand as a business owner.

According to the courts, a shareholder must meet two basic requirements to have an adjusted basis for a loan to an S Corporation. The first and most basic requirement is that the debt is owed directly by the S Corporation to the shareholder. If a shareholder simply guarantees the S-debt, Corporation's the shareholder does not have a basis in debt to the S Corporation. [14] The shareholder must also have an actual "economic outlay," according to the second requirement.

In addition to cash, you may have contributed property such as a computer, automobile, tools, or other items. The shareholder basis would rise due to capital contributions, ordinary income, investment income, and gains. Basis decreases include charitable contributions, Section 179 depreciation (accelerated depreciation), non-deductible expenses such as shareholder life insurance, one-half of meals and entertainment, tax penalties, net losses, and shareholder distributions. Basis adjustments are usually calculated at the end of a company's fiscal year.

These changes to the property's foundation must be made in a specific order. First, any income items such as ordinary income, dividend income, interest earned, passive income, and capital gains would be added to any basis. Distributions reduce the basis, followed by deduction, loss items, and current losses.

Consider stock basis the same way you would consider a bank account. Any deposits and the interest income the bank pays will be credited to your bank account. Inflows of cash, equipment, and profit would accompany stock basis deposits. A deduction from your bank account is money taken out for yourself, money used to pay bills, and fees you must pay. A decrease in stock basis would be any profit distributions you took for yourself and any expenses you paid on behalf of the corporation. Your basis, like a bank account, can never fall below zero. We can talk about reasonable compensation and distributions now that we know the basics.

A substantial amount of compensation to be packaged for an S Corporation shareholder is most likely one of the rifts in the Tax Code that has been abused. When explaining to a client why they should be taxed as an S Corporation, we would tell them that S Corporations are flow-through entities, which means that when profits flow over to the shareholder, they are not subject to self-employment tax. However, this is an incorrect statement that should be investigated immediately. S Corporation shareholders must be fairly compensated. As a result, a portion of their compensation is subject to FICA taxes, which are simply another name for self-employment tax. However, the theory guiding the introduction of the S-Election is that a shareholder can only choose what they pay self-employment tax on because it is only paid through FICA taxes and reasonable compensation. What constitutes fair compensation, then?

According to Internal Revenue Service policy, distributions from S Corporations can be classified as compensation and subject to FICA taxes. This policy, supported by several Revenue Procedures (Rev. Proc.) on the subject, is comprehensive in scope, and the Courts were left to decide how to interpret the Service's stance.

Following an audit, the IRS determined that all payments to the shareholder were compensation and assessed FICA taxes on the amount taken. In this case, the company agreed that the sole shareholder would be an employee. During a recession, the shareholder moved personal funds from their bank account to the company's bank account. Glass Blocks complained that the payments made to the sole shareholder were simply loan repayments. The IRS responded to their claim by claiming that the funds transferred were capital contributions and that the distributions received by the shareholder were compensation. The United States Tax Court requested evidence to prove that the funds transferred were loans made by the taxpayer. The court later determined that four factors contradicted the company's claim that the funds were loans.

The court determined that there was no promissory note or written agreement between the shareholder and the company regarding a loan from the shareholder; no interest was charged to the company on the repayment; no security was provided for the loan, and there was no amortization schedule of fixed repayments for the loan.

The company would have a dividend payment policy if the shareholder-owned stock in any corporation with earnings. Most public companies, for example, report quarterly earnings. Dividends are usually paid quarterly if they pay them.

As practitioners, we are unlikely to deal with publicly traded companies, but a distribution policy must be in place. Profit distributions in the policy can be specified to be paid monthly, quarterly, or yearly. Because no other corporation pays dividends in this manner, a shareholder cannot receive distributions at arbitrary intervals such as weekly or biweekly. In addition, the IRS could rule that a weekly or biweekly distribution payment is a disguised salary. As a result, they are required to pay FICA taxes.

To summarize, determining fair compensation for an S-shareholder corporation is difficult. However, we have discovered some guidelines that we can follow. For example, it's clear from the examples above that fair compensation doesn't just happen; it varies by company. A client's condition does not always apply to another. Unfortunately for them, there are no simple solutions for determining what is reasonable compensation. Simply put, we must approach each business differently. Owners of S Corporations who perform services for the corporation must be fairly compensated for their efforts.

Chapter 7: Taxes and How to Fill Them

The S Corporation has made a special election with the IRS and is now taxed as an LLC or partnership. As a result, an S Corporation is not subject to corporate income tax, and its earnings are taxed "pass-through," which means that the company's profits or losses are passed through to the shareholders or owners. As a result, S Corporation's earnings are not taxed twice.

An S Corporation protects its owners from liability while avoiding federal income taxation. It is a type of corporation found in IRC Subchapter S of Chapter 1.

The first step in forming an S Corporation is to incorporate it as a regular corporation. To do so, you must file and submit certain documents, such as a certificate of incorporation and articles of incorporation, with the SEC or another government agency. You will also be required to pay the fees of the institutions.

To obtain the S Corporation designation, you and all other stockholders must sign Form 2553 after successfully incorporating your company. Income taxes will be filed and paid individually by you and all other owners on your returns following the successful tax identification of your business as an S Corporation.

To qualify, your corporation must meet the following requirements, according to the Internal Revenue Service:

- It must be based or domiciled in the United States.

- It must have only allowable stockholders, including individuals, estates, and specific types of trusts. It must exclude non-resident alien stockholders and business entities such as partnerships and corporations.

- It must have only allowable stockholders.

- The total number of stockholders cannot exceed 100.

- The company must have only one stock classification.

- It cannot be a disqualified corporation under the S Corp structure, such as certain types of financial institutions, domestic and international sales corporations, or insurance companies.

How are S Corporation Shareholders Taxed?

The shareholders report their income/losses on individual tax returns and pay any required income tax at their tax rates. An S Corporation with two or more shareholders is taxed similarly to a partnership. In contrast, an S Corporation with one shareholder is taxed similarly to a sole proprietorship. An S Corporation does not pay federal income tax at the corporate level.

1120S IRS Form

IRS Form 1120S is completed and filed by an S corporation (US Corporation Income Tax Return for an S Corporation). Form 1120S is merely an informational return in which the S Corporation discloses its income and losses for the tax year, as well as the allocable share of the income and losses for each of its shareholders.

K-1 Schedule

In addition to filing Form 1120S, the S Corporation sends a Schedule K-1 (Shareholder's Share of Income, Credits, and Deductions) to each shareholder.

Tax Consequences of Allocated vs. Distributed Shares

The Schedule K-1 for each shareholder contains specific information about the shareholder's allocable share of the S-income corporation and deductions. Each shareholder must then report these figures on their tax return (IRS Form 1040) and pay tax on their share of the S-income corporation regardless of whether the income was distributed to the shareholder.

Profits and losses of the S Corporation are allocated based on the percentage of ownership interest in the S Corporation and retained earnings.

Although an S Corporation can keep its profits as retained earnings, those earnings are taxed. On the other hand, retained earnings of a C-corporation are not taxed until they are distributed as dividends, salaries, or bonuses.

When an S Corporation makes a profit during the tax year, it does not have to pay corporate income tax on that profit. Instead, it can pay out some of its profits as dividends to shareholders, reinvest some of its profits as retained earnings, or do both.

Because the S Corporation is a pass-through entity, its profits are passed through to its shareholders, and all of the S-net corporation's profits are taxable to the S-shareholders. In other words, whether the S Corporation distributes profits to shareholders as dividends, keeps profits for itself as retained earnings, or does a little of both, S Corporation shareholders pay tax on the S-net corporation's profit. But take note of two things:

If the S Corporation distributes profits to its shareholders (as dividends), they do not have to pay tax on that distribution. However, if the company retains the profits, the shareholders must still pay income taxes on all of the S-profits Corporation (which includes the retained earnings).

In other words, the S-shareholders corporation pays income tax on money (retained earnings) that they never received (and will never receive directly) because retained earnings are money retained by the S Corporation to be used for future reasonable business activities.

How to Avoid Double Taxation

To avoid being taxed twice on the same income, it is critical to understand what the IRS says about an S Corporation regarding federal income taxation.

Many investors consider this to be one of the property's most desirable features because a regular corporation's taxable income is subject to double taxation. The first occurs at the corporate level, while the second occurs at the individual level in the form of stockholder dividend income taxes.

In the earlier chapter on LLCs, you saw how double taxation on a regular corporation looks. The pass-through income taxation scheme eliminates double taxation if you choose to incorporate as an S Corporation. Because its profits and losses are reported on the individual tax returns of its shareholders, an S Corp is exempt from paying income taxes.

This benefit, however, is not available to all S Corps. Some states and municipalities have enacted legislation that denies such advantages to these businesses.

Take, for example, the city of New York. The city imposes an 8.85% corporate income tax on S Corporations. However, if the corporation can show that it operates outside New York, its income will be exempt from this flat rate. Similarly, California imposes a franchise tax of 1.5% of an S Corporation's annual net income or $800, whichever is greater.

Form 1120S will be used to file your income tax return if you choose an S Corporation; Profits, losses, and deductions of shareholders are itemized on Schedule K-1, just like they are for LLCs.

For tax purposes, the IRS regards an S Corp as a simple pass-through entity. This means that taxes on its income are eventually passed down to its owners for them to pay income taxes. Except for that, this business entity operates similarly to regular corporations.

Many states use federal data on taxpayers' total income to calculate state taxes. As a result, it is critical to file and pay federal income taxes correctly.

You pay income taxes as an S Corporation owner based on your distributive share of the company's net income. If you have a single LLC and have elected to be one, you own the entire net income. These taxes will be reported on Form 1040.

Double taxation is one of the most common complaints about a regular corporation. While the law prohibits double taxation on individuals, double taxation on regular corporation income applies to two different parties. An S Corporation does not have this problem. Because it is only a pass-through entity for tax purposes, its income is taxed as the owners' income. Unlike regular corporations, which are taxed at corporate and personal income levels due to dividends, S Corp income is taxed only once.

Taxes on Self-Employment

Dividends are paid to shareholders of a regular corporation in exchange for their investment. However, S Corp owners must pay regular income taxes on their share of the company's earnings, but the IRS does not consider them self-employed. As a result, you will not have to pay self-employment taxes on your portion of the company's income. However, if you work for the company and receive a salary, you must pay FICA or self-employment taxes such as Social Security and Medicare. As a result, S Corp owner-employees are subject to this tax.

Other S Corporation Taxes

Your S Corporation will have to pay other business taxes like any other business. These are employment or payroll taxes, state-imposed excise and sales taxes, and state-specific taxes on S Corps such as gross receipts, franchise, and income taxes.

How Much Can Small Businesses Earn Before Taxes?

According to the IRS, all businesses, except partnerships, must file an annual income tax return. Partnerships must file an information return. You must pay employment taxes if you have employees.

Business owners who earn less than $400 in profits are exempt from the self-employment tax, which is the only tax you can avoid. The IRS is unlikely to audit your small business until it starts making money. Even if you are losing money, filing your taxes is essential to avoid legal problems and take advantage of deductions.

When Should You Pay Small Business Taxes?

As important as the types of taxes you must pay, you must also consider when you must pay them. Many business owners pay their taxes only once before the IRS's deadline. However, many business owners must regularly pay estimated self-employment and income taxes.

The estimated tax is the tax you pay throughout the year based on your estimated taxable income. According to the IRS, business owners, including sole proprietors, stockholders, and partners, should make quarterly estimated tax payments if they believe they will owe $1000 or more in taxes when their federal or state tax returns are filed.

Form 1040-ES can be used to calculate your estimated taxes. You can also use your previous year's income, tax deductions, and credits as a starting point. Another helpful resource is last year's federal tax return. When filing your tax return, you can deduct the estimated tax payments you made throughout the year from your total liability. The federal income tax is a "pay-as-you-go" tax, which means that if you don't make the required payments when they're due, you'll have to pay interest and penalties.

After you figure out the number and e-file the tax form, you have several options for paying the IRS: IRS Pay By Card, which allows you to pay with a debit or credit card online, or IRS Direct Pay, which allows the IRS to deduct the money you owe from your checking (or savings) account. You can also pay the IRS over the phone.

The quarterly estimated tax payments for every respective quarter are due every April 15th, June 15th, Sept 15th, and Jan 15th of the following year.

Quarterly Estimated Tax Due Date

Period You Get Paid	Tax Due Date
January 1– March 31	April 15
April 1– May 31	June 15
June 1– August 31	September 15
September 1– December 31	January 15 of the following year

In contrast to salaried employees, whose employers withhold a certain amount of tax from each paycheck, freelancers, sole proprietors, and business owners bear the entire tax burden.

Furthermore, individuals who are partners in corporations are frequently required to pay quarterly taxes if they estimate they owe at least $500 in taxes.

On the other hand, business owners who fail to submit at least 90% of their owed taxes face severe penalties. As a result, working with a tax professional who can double-check the amount owed is recommended.

How Tax Deductions and Credits Affect Your Business Tax Rate

As previously stated, with the 20% deduction available to sole proprietors and other pass-through entities, determining your business's final tax rate is more complicated than simply multiplying net income by your tax rate. The following is a brief overview of three factors that influence your final tax bill (and we will discuss them in detail in later sections).

- **Operating Losses (Net):** Some businesses may have a net operating loss deduction carried forward from the previous year to reduce the amount of taxable income in the current year.

- **Deductions for taxes:** Many business owners want to take advantage of tax breaks to reduce their taxable income. Yes, some deductions can have a significant impact on your bottom line. For example, the Section 179 deduction allows businesses to deduct the total cost of an asset, such as machinery or a vehicle, in the year of purchase.

- **Tax Credits:** Many businesses qualify for tax credits, reducing the tax amount they must pay. In some ways, tax credits are superior to tax deductions because they allow you to deduct the amount of tax owed on a dollar-for-dollar basis. For example, a company that uses alternative energy or fuel may be eligible for the tax credit.

Because of the tax breaks and credits, two businesses with the same net income from the previous year can pay different federal income taxes.

On Average, How Much Tax Do Small Businesses Pay?

According to Small Business Administration data, small businesses of all types pay an average tax rate of about 19.8%. Small businesses with one owner pay an average tax rate of 13.3%, while those with more than one owner pay an average tax rate of 23.6%. Small S corporations pay an average tax rate of 26.9%.

Because they have earned more money, some corporations have higher tax rates. That makes sense when you consider that 18% of small S corporations earn $100,000 or more in net income, but nearly 60% of small businesses with one owner earn less than $10,000.

How to Handle Business Taxes

You now understand what your company can expect from the tax, and you may be wondering how to prepare so that you are not caught off guard when it comes time to pay your taxes. Because no two businesses pay the same amount of tax, each approach will be slightly different.

Any business owner can do the best for their company to save money ahead of time. Set aside 30-40% of your quarterly income to cover federal and state taxes, preferably at the rate applicable to your small business. It is especially important when you have just started your business and do not yet understand your company's tax liabilities.

As you save your tax refund:

1. Are you new to the world of small business? Set aside at least 30% of your pay every time you get paid.

2. Have you recently made a profit? Then save your 30% monthly.

3. Is your profit reasonably consistent year after year? Consider dividing your net income from last year by four. Take 30% of that figure and try to save that much every quarter.

Another good practice is to keep tax money separate in a business bank. This way, you won't squander money that could have gone to the IRS. You can also set up automatic transfers from your business bank account to another separate account (quarterly or monthly) to ensure that you save enough money to cover your tax bill.

You shouldn't be concerned about underpaying or miscalculating the amount owed. According to the IRS, if you pay the same amount in taxes each quarter as you did the previous year, you are protected by the "safe harbor rule," which states that you will not be penalized for underpayment.

For more about this rule, you can read on the **IRS website** (https://www.irs.gov/taxtopics/tc306)

Chapter 8: S Corporation Mistakes and How to Avoid Them

Excessive Overhead

Overhead can quickly become unmanageable, especially given the limited number of requirements for effective freight broker agents. Computers, phones, and occasional travel are required, but they can be used in any room, from a living room to a small, basic office.

While modern technologies are beneficial, costs and budgetary constraints must be considered. Self-employed agents must exercise caution regarding expenses such as software, bookkeeping, and time-consuming administrative tasks.

Failure to Evolve

A wide range of additional skills is required to run a successful business. Agents who want to grow their business often find it difficult because hiring full-time employees for back-office assistance and other tasks is such a risk.

Even in an increasingly high-tech environment, S Corporation issues can be addressed by employing tried-and-true low-tech techniques such as well-targeted phone follow-ups and lightning-fast customer service.

Complacency

For a regular business, there is a lot of competition. The thing to avoid is looking for new ways to improve it. Someone will always be able to do things differently and possibly better. A successful businessperson is always looking for ways to improve.

Not Embracing Technology

You may have heard of this thing called the Internet. Intelligent companies, including freight brokers, have fully embraced technology. Technology can assist you in shortening processes and automating routine tasks. As a result, you will have more time to devote to your business's marketing and other revenue-generating aspects.

In contrast, installing processes entails defining clear workflows so that your employees fully understand what is expected of them in a situation. Many business owners believe that their employees are equally capable of dealing with volatile situations. This, however, is not always the case. You may have had to learn how to do things from the ground up; expecting your employees to do the same is a waste of time.

Instead, use technology to automate the most unimportant tasks and create good documentation that instructs your employees on what to do in various situations. They can then improve those processes by building on them. Returning to technology, successful freight brokers make use of a variety of software programs.

To handle bookkeeping and accounting, you'll need software. This is a must-have for all businesses. Don't mistake saving paper receipts and manually entering them into a spreadsheet. Invest in high-quality software, and you will undoubtedly reap the benefits in the long run.

Inadequate Funding

Always ensure that you have enough cash in the bank and are adequately capitalized. If you aren't, you're on your way to a life of agony in which every business decision feels like pulling teeth. In your personal life, imagine having to choose between food and water because you only have enough money for one expense.

That may appear absurd, but many business owners put themselves and their companies in this position by being naive. Fortunately, you are not naive because you are reading this book and educating yourself. On the other hand, undercapitalization puts even the most promising businesses out of work.

When starting a business, most owners try to save as much money as possible. This is understandable given the low cash flow and high costs. However, there is a distinction between cutting costs and shooting yourself in the foot. You should bootstrap your operations to the greatest extent possible, but not so far that you can't afford to buy the tools you need to succeed.

The profit equation has two components: costs and revenues. Many businesses concentrate solely on costs, believing revenues will care for themselves. To generate revenue, however, you must actively invest money. Take note that I said "invest" rather than "spend." Purchasing software is an investment that will pay for itself many times over in utility.

Similarly, hiring and paying great employees who will generate revenue for you is an investment rather than an expense. As a business owner, your primary goal is to allocate capital. Your employees will be able to manage the day-to-day operations of the company.

However, they will only be able to do so efficiently if you provide them with the necessary resources to do a good job. If you don't do this, it's akin to purchasing a high-end sports car, refusing to fill the tank with premium fuel, or avoiding long-lasting purchasing tires.

Ineffective Procedures and Processes

A process distinguishes a one-person operation from a large corporation. When you hire even one person, you are responsible for assisting them in carrying out their responsibilities effectively. They must perform well and earn more than you do.

No technology allows people to transfer their thoughts to another person directly, and your employee is unlikely to be a mind reader. The only thing you can do to help them is to create as many standardized processes as possible and procedures that can be repeated repeatedly.

As a business owner, you will spend most of your time refining and tuning your processes to ensure everything runs smoothly. You'll spend your entire day putting out fires if you don't. So, focus on developing highly repeatable processes that even inexperienced employees can understand; don't leave loose ends, and document everything. This is what will assist you in growing your business.

Narrow Business Book

This error occurs because these business owners do not consider marketing a continuous activity as important as operations. There will be no operations if there is no marketing. Marketing is more important than operations regarding freight brokerage because your customers are always looking for brokers who can offer them lower rates.

Your competitors will always try to entice your customers away from you. While providing excellent service is a perfect way to keep them on board with you, it does not protect you from the customer's business failing. You must constantly advertise yourself and implement strong marketing processes to keep your company at the forefront of every customer's mind.

You'll have a complete marketing strategy ready when you're finished. Understand, however, that even the best marketing plans require your commitment and desire. You will struggle if you're unwilling to invest the same energy in marketing as you do in your operations.

Dead Invoices

Dead invoices are a common issue in the freight brokerage industry. Your customers typically pay you after 60 days, whereas your suppliers expect payment within 30 days. This results in a cash-flow gap. You can easily overcome this obstacle if your book of business is strong. However, new businesses rarely have large customer bases that they can rely on.

Most customers will treat you according to your expectations. If you do not communicate your terms and payment process, they will most likely take advantage of you and delay payment. When you combine this situation with a limited business book, you have a recipe for disaster.

It is your processes that will save you. It makes sense to automate invoice tracking and collection as much as possible. Automation is expensive, but you're less likely to miss payments due to poor cash reconciliation to invoices or lose a customer dispute because you couldn't pull up a record in time. It all comes down to how much money you're willing to put up. Most business owners do not consider invoice and payment collection worthwhile investment areas, assuming it will happen automatically once the job is completed.

You must, however, constantly negotiate credit cycles and work to maximize cash flow. Allowing your invoices to collect dust is a sure way never to get paid. The key is to develop processes that allow you to efficiently collect payments and follow up with your customers on time. Dispute resolution should be accompanied by processes allowing your employees to track and resolve disputes quickly.

Focusing Solely on the Money

Because you're in business to make money, it's natural that you'll be concerned about the financial aspects of each load that comes your way. Many newcomers enter these transactions without considering the consequences of their actions. There is no such thing as a free lunch in this industry, and there is always a catch with such loads.

Prioritize relationships while keeping monetary terms fair to all parties. You may have to give up a few margin points here and there, but that doesn't mean you have to cripple yourself to succeed in this business. Everyone you deal with will try to drive a hard bargain, but that's normal. Everyone benefits from the best deals. That is what keeps people returning to you. So, concentrate on the value you can offer people, and you'll have no trouble making money.

Chapter 9: Deduction Tactics

The tax deduction, also known as the "tax write-off," is an expense that can be deducted from your taxable income. You take your business expenses and deduct them from your income. It only allows you to pay a lower tax bill, and the deducted expenses must meet IRS tax deduction criteria.

How to Claim Business Startup Tax Breaks

Even if you can deduct some of your business's startup costs, there are some limitations. Business expenses are limited to $5,000 in deductions during the first year of operation. As a result, if your startup costs more than $50,000, your first-year tax deduction will be reduced by more than $50,000.

For example, if your startup costs $52,000, your first-year deductions will be reduced by $2,000, bringing the total to $3,000. You will lose the entire deduction if your expenses exceed $55,000. The remaining costs can then be amortized and deducted over 15 years, beginning with the second operation year.

How to Claim Business Startup Deductions on Tax Returns

You must report the first-year deduction on your business tax form if you take it. Schedule C is for sole proprietors, Form 1120 is for corporations, and K-1 is for a partnership or S corporation. The amortized deductions can be claimed on Form 4562 in subsequent years (Depreciation and Amortization).

The deduction is then carried over to your Schedule C under other business expenses if you are a sole proprietor or to the corporate or partnership income tax form if you are a corporation or partnership. You can then continue to claim it for the remainder of the amortization period.

Top Small Business Tax Breaks

The following are the most common business expenses that can be deducted. Keep this checklist in mind when attempting to deduct business taxes. Please remember that some of the deductions may not apply to your business. Consult your CPA or tax advisor before claiming them.

Promotion and Advertising

Advertising and promotion costs are entirely deductible. The cost of printing business brochures and cards; hiring someone to design your business logo; purchasing ad space in online media or print; launching a new website; sending cards to clients; sponsoring an event; and running a social media marketing campaign are all included in this category.

However, money paid to sponsor political events or campaigns, or to influence legislation, cannot be deducted (such as lobbying)

Commercial Insurance

You can deduct the premiums paid for business insurance, which may include:

- Liability coverage.
- Property coverage for your furniture, buildings, and equipment.

- Group health, vision, and dental insurance for your employees.

- Workers' compensation coverage.

- Malpractice insurance or professional liability.

- Auto insurance for your business vehicle.

- Business interruption insurance covers losses if your business is forced to close due to a fire or other unforeseen event.

Business Meals

Generally, you can deduct half of the qualifying costs for food and beverages. To be eligible for this deduction, you must:

- The meals cannot be extravagant under the circumstances; the expenses must be a necessary and ordinary part of doing business, and the employee or business owners must be present at the meals.

- You can also deduct 50% of your employees' meals, such as buying burgers for dinner if your team works late. Meals provided at office picnics and parties are also fully deductible.

- Maintain documentation demonstrating the date and location of the meal, the amount of each expense, and the business relationship of the individual with whom you dined.

Write the purpose of the meal and any other relevant information on the back of the receipt.

Commercial Use of Your Vehicle

Do you use your vehicle for business purposes? You can deduct the entire operating cost if you only use your vehicle for business purposes. You can only deduct business-related expenses when you use them for personal and business trips.

Bank Charges

Having separate credit cards and bank accounts for your business is always a good idea. Monthly or annual service fees, overdraft fees, and transfer fees assessed by your credit card or bank are tax deductible. Transactions or merchant fees paid to a third-party payment processor can also be deducted (i.e., Stripe or PayPal). On the other hand, fees for personal credit or bank accounts are not deductible.

Contract Labor

You can deduct their fees as business expenses if you hire independent contractors or freelancers to help you with your business. If you pay a contractor more than $600 during the tax year, you must send them a Form 1099-NEC by January 31st.

Education Expenses

Education expenses are fully deductible because they increase your expertise and add value to your business. To determine whether your workshop or class qualifies, the IRS considers whether the expenses maintain or improve the skills required in your current business.

Depreciation

Suppose you purchased equipment, furniture, or other business assets. In that case, depreciation rules require you to spread the expenses of those assets over the years you will use them rather than deducting the entire amount in a single hit.

Rental Cost

You can deduct the rental payments if you rent business equipment or a location for your business. Even if you have a home office, remember that rent paid on your home cannot be deducted as a business expense. However, the rent can be deducted from the home office expense. For more information, please see the following item.

Personal Tax Breaks for Business Owners

Aside from the deductions mentioned above, you can claim on Form 1065 for Schedule C, and there are a couple of tax breaks that small business owners commonly claim on their tax returns.

Health-Care Costs

Aside from insurance premiums, some out-of-pocket medical expenses are deductible and itemized on Schedule A, such as office copays and prescription drug costs.

On Schedule 1 of Form 1040, self-employed business owners can deduct health insurance premiums for themselves and dependents (such as their spouse). You cannot, however, deduct health care premiums if you can participate in a plan through your spouse's employer.

Donations to Charities

Charitable contributions cannot be deducted as business expenses by LLCs, sole proprietorships, or partners. The deductions, however, may be claimed on the business owners' tax returns. Donations must be made to qualified organizations to qualify.

Cash contributions can be claimed as "above-the-line" deductions on Form 1040. If you want to deduct more than the limit (in 2020, taxpayers could claim up to $300), you can itemize your deductions on Schedule A, which is attached to Form 1040.

Contributions to Retirement Plans

Employee retirement contributions can also be deducted as a business expense. If you only contribute to your retirement accounts, you can claim the contribution on Schedule 1 and attach it to Form 1040. Your plan type determines the amount you can deduct. Following the IRS's instructions, you can calculate your retirement plan contribution and deduction.

Expenses for Child and Dependent Care

If you pay someone to care for your child or another dependent while working, you may be eligible for the child and dependent care credit. To be eligible, the person receiving care must be a 13-year-old child, your spouse, or any other dependents who are mentally or physically incapable of self-care.

The credit will be worth approximately 20-35% of your allowable expenses based on your income. In addition, allowable costs are limited to $3,000 for one dependent and $6,000 for more than two dependents. IRS Publication 503 contains more information on the child and dependent care credit. Remember to include Form 2441 with your Form 1040 to claim it.

The Complete Tax Deduction

So, what exactly is a 100% tax deduction? It is a business expense that can be completely deducted from your taxable income taxes. For small businesses, the following expenses are completely deductible:

- Office supplies, such as printers, scanners, and computers; Furniture purchased solely for office use in the year of purchase.

- Employee and client gifts, up to $25 per person per year.

- Business travel and related expenses, such as hotels and car rentals.

- Yearly business phone bills.

- If you are self-employed, pay your health insurance premiums, which are fully deductible.

How to Claim Tax Breaks as a Business Owner

You must complete a Schedule C tax form to claim small-business tax deductions as a sole proprietorship. The taxable income for the year is calculated using Form Schedule C. Report this profit and calculate the taxes owed on your personal 1040 form.

Understandably, no one wants to pay taxes or the tax filing fee. Tax deductions are an important tool for lowering the amount of tax owed. Even if the IRS comes knocking, keeping good records will help you get those deductions. If you have any questions about your business tax return, always seek the advice of a tax professional.

Conclusion

Thank you for taking the time to read this book. A small business may benefit significantly from being an S Corp. This is due to its ability to issue a wide range of stocks with virtually no restrictions on who can own shares and a virtually unlimited number of shareholders. An S Corporation's profits are not taxed. However, filing a tax return with the IRS using Form 1120S is required, as is providing Form K-1 to all members to report income when filing individual tax returns.

One critical requirement is that an S Corporation pays its shareholders who work for the company a reasonable salary. If the company did not pay its employees' salaries at fair market value, the IRS might reclassify the shareholder's distribution as "wages."

Because states treat S Corporations similarly to the IRS, most states do not tax their profits. However, some states tax S Corporations at the corporate and shareholder levels.

S corporations are notoriously difficult for business owners to grasp (and the pass-through concept overall). It can be perplexing to pay personal income tax on a corporation's profits when the owner does not receive them in cash. The inverse relationship between the owner's wages and the corporation's taxable profits can also be perplexing. On the other hand, the FICA tax savings are difficult to beat and are the primary reason for S corporations' popularity.

Good luck!

Made in the USA
Las Vegas, NV
30 November 2023

81764687R00059